All the Thoughts Inside My Head

Raylene Plummer

Presentation by *BookLeaf Publishing*

Web: www.bookleafpub.com

E-mail: info@bookleafpub.com

ISBN: 9789357214056

First edition 2023

To my ever supportive husband Matt who has brought me numerous notebooks and pens as he has had the belief in me as a writer.

If You Can Pick Up a Pen You Can Write!

A flicker, a spark, somewhere deep inside.
If you can pick up a pen you can write.

A word, then more, drawn to each other.
If you can pick up a pen you can write.

An inner monologue, listen to that voice.
If you can pick up a pen you can write.

A pen, a tool, your most powerful weapon.
If you can pick up a pen you can write.

Paper, crisp, smooth and white.
If you can pick up a pen you can write.

A hand assesses, caresses the pen.
If you can pick up a pen you can write.

A test of comfort, glide and style.
If you can pick up a pen you can write.

Words stand out on that crisp, white page.
If you can pick up a pen you can write.

Like a torrent, they fall, from head to paper.
If you can pick up a pen you can write.

Pace gathers, quickens, as they race to be heard.
If you can pick up a pen you can write.

An outtake of breath, relief washes over.
If you can pick up a pen you can write.

Belief in yourself on the page in front of you.
I can pick up a pen I can write!

40

I spy with my little eye,
Someone who's turning forty.

Wrinkles and creases,
Bags under the eyes,

I spy with my little eye,
Someone who's turning forty.

A layer of fat hides once tighter abs,
Calorie counting and keeping tabs.

I spy with my little eye,
Someone who's turning forty.

Eleven o'clock is now a late night
3am parties no longer in sight.

I spy with my little eye,
Someone who's turning forty.

Sauvignon blanc replaces cheap wine,
Now handles their drink, a positive sign.

I spy with my little eye,
Someone who's turning forty.

Married with kids, dogs and some cats,
Never succumbed to getting pet rats.

I spy with my little eye,
Someone who's turning forty.

Odd nights out for a meal and a drink,
Brain-fog in waves, struggling to think.

I spy with my little eye,
Someone who's turning forty.

Joggers, a hoodie, no make-up on,
The need to impress, most definitely gone.

I spy with my little eye,
Someone who's turning forty.

Watches, 'Location, Location,' 'A Farm in the
Dales,'
Yet still gets excited by those 'Magic Mike'
males,

I spy with my little eye,
Someone who's turning forty.

The most content they've been in their life,
Fulfillment in being a mother, a wife.

I spy with my little eye,
Someone who's turning forty.

Copes better with forty than thirty for sure,
Though knows fifty soon, will knock at the door.

I spy with my little eye,
Someone who's turning forty.

Looks forward to the future, fondly on the past,
Hoping their memory will last and last.

I spy with my little eye,
Someone who's turning forty.

What if?

What if the world was flat instead of round?
Would the end of the earth, ever be found?

What if fruit was bad but chocolate good?
Would chocolate still be, your favourite food?

What if day was dark but night was light?
Would the mean old bogeyman, still give you a
fright?

What if men could give birth, instead of women?
Would the world see more or much less
children?

What if you could marry someone, living or
dead?
Would you choose with your heart, or choose
with your head?

What if you could travel, back in time?
Would you stop a murder or another crime?

What if you could travel, to the future?
Would you adapt or walk around in a stupor?

What if you could sacrifice yourself for
humanity?
Would you deem it necessary or a profanity?

What if you needed, no sleep at all?
Would you party all night, having a ball?

What if a genie, gave you three wishes?
Would you live a modest life, or one filled with
riches?

What if this life, is just a test?
Would it fill you with hope, or a feeling of
unrest?

Tinsel

Shiny, garish,
Frantically, chaotically, imperfectly,
Twinkling, turning, twisting, twirling.

Christmas

Cherished
Happy
Real
Inspiring
Sparkling
Thoughtful
Magical
Amazing
Sweet

Mug

The morning air is filled with cries,
Of angry children with wild eyes,
"Idiot, pig, you little poo,
I'll knock your head off, see that I do."

But where is Mum in all of this?
Believe me, not in a place of bliss.
For Mum has risen feeling grotty,
Headache, sore throat, nose all snotty.

Yet up she gets to heat the pan,
Nutella pancakes for the clan.
And toast for the one with different tastes,
She fills the dishwasher, no time to waste.

Then feed the chickens, dogs and cat,
Whilst the children eat with their bottoms sat,
At the breakfast bar where they are moaning,
Of coughs and aches, even tummies are
groaning.

They really, really can't go to school,
Although they know that it's the rule,
That every child in our land,
Has the privilege to be educated first hand.

But alas, this goes right over their heads,
For they'd prefer to be in their beds.
Ipads, Xbox or the TV,
Is as far as their snotty noses can see.

Next we encounter the daily struggle,
Of getting dressed for these poor muggles.
They cannot possibly do this on their own,
Instead they'd rather gripe and moan.

"Why can't you dress me? Come on Mum."
"What next?" I ask myself. "Wipe your bum?"
All this is said with voices high,
If I had time, I'd sit and cry.

Instead I try to keep the peace,
Which falls on deaf ears so I release,
Myself from the fight and from despair,
I try to stay calm, breathing in air.

And take myself off to defrost the car,
Rest be assured, my ear is not far,
From the persistent bickering of my eldest two,
In these situations they know what to do.

But rather than follow their mother's advice,
They'd rather say and do things that aren't nice.
Eventually we're in the car, ready to go,
Eldest shouting "Turn off the radio!"

Inside my stomach is bubbling and churning,
As I realise deep down that all I am yearning,
Is calm and respect, understanding and love.
Is it so hard to achieve the above?

We arrive at school, and off they go,
Angelic faces, shouting "Hello",
To friends whom they play with, nothing amiss,
"Un-believable," under my breath I hiss.

Day in and out I do my best,
When do I get a chance to rest?
What this Mum needs is a big, fat hug,
For today this Mum really feels like a mug!

I Hate You

I hate you,
Three words,
Only three words.
Three words said in anger.
In frustration.
No excuses,
Those words hurt.
The first time you hear them,
A tiny fracture.
You brush it off.
It's a niggle.
You pride your strength,
Your resilience.
The second time.
No longer a niggle.
A twinge.
It takes more healing.
But the crack is still there,
A gentle reminder.
The third time.
A wrench.
It brings tears to your eyes.
You wipe them away.
The fourth time.
A break.

You sob.
Pain washes over you.
You feel it in your stomach.
Nauseous.
This time takes longer to heal.
Until the next time.
A crack that can't be papered.
Words that have left a permanent scar.
Hate from the one you love most.

Grandpa

Mum saw a butterfly float past,
It reminded her of you.
Maybe you're watching over us,
I hope that it is true.

This poem is my memories,
Of a truly wonderful man.
A husband, dad and grandpa,
I'll do the best I can.

I loved when you told a story,
You'd hook your finger round,
Give it a shake and tilt you head,
Your laugh was a beautiful sound.

I loved how every Christmas,
You'd join in with Chase the Ace,
And how you'd let the children win,
To save them losing face.

I loved how you loved your great grandkids,
Caring about their well-being.
To know they've grown up with you in their life,
Is really a wonderful feeling.

I loved how you cared for our husbands,
Even though they weren't your blood.
Chatting about work or the football,
Or just generally chewing the cud.

I loved how much you loved Nannie,
She really was your life.
To me you really epitomised,
What it meant to be husband and wife.

I loved you were a creature of habit,
Every lunchtime you'd have a beer,
Well buttered bread, a pack of plain crisps,
A whisky for good cheer.

I loved trying to give you a hug,
It didn't come naturally to you.
You'd be stiff as a board, you wouldn't relax,
But it didn't stop us wanting to.

I even loved when you were cranky.
I wouldn't know whether to laugh or to cry.
Because sometimes that was just you,
From the cast that you were die.

The tears that now fall from our eyes,
Is love with no place to go.
We miss you more than words can say,
And love you more than you can know.

Silent Monster

Silent, stealthily, it sneaks up on you.
You sometimes feel it coming,
The knot in the chest, the shortness of breath.
Other times it beats you to it.
Ba boom, ba boom, ba boom,
The extra flutter of the heart,
Enough to make you stop and think,
Have I had caffeine?
You know you haven't,
This knowing makes it worse,
Breath in....
And out......
And in......
Close your mind off,
It's playing tricks on you.
Listen out for five things,
Pinch your fingers,
Focus your breath.
But, still, it keeps coming.
It's tentacles far reaching,
Reminding you it's there.
Palpitations.
Suddenly, an overwhelming sense you're
struggling for breath.
It's reached its climax.

You're left, ragged breath, clammy skin.
Afraid to sleep yet tired.
So fucking tired.
You start to drift,
Breathing slows.
A small tap that causes you to inhale,
Still there, dormant but very much alive.
It is strong.
You must be stronger.
Fuck you!
Until next time, it whispers.

The Airport

Hustle, bustle,
Packets rustle,
Here inside the airport.

Frazzled, bedazzled,
Parents hassled,
Here inside the airport.

Pushing, rushing,
Lovers gushing,
Here inside the airport.

Crying, sighing,
Airplanes flying,
Here inside the airport.

Eating, meeting,
Lounging on seating,
Here inside the airport.

Thinking, winking,
Youngsters drinking.
Here inside the airport.

Shopping, stopping,
People watching.
Here inside the airport.

Care-free, make-up free,
All important duty-free.
Here inside the airport.

Happily, nervously,
Waiting excitedly.
Here inside the airport.

A Holiday in the Sun

Sandy toes,
Sunburned nose,
Salty kisses,
Darting fishes,
Iced tea,
Aqua sea,
Crystal pool,
Karaoke fool,
Lazy days,
Purple haze,
Sights a must,
Wanderlust.

Flames

Warm, carefree,
Flickering, dancing, licking,
Energetically, wildly, dangerously, effortlessly.

Snow

Soft, White,
Gently, Softly, Slowly,
Falling, Laying, Coating, Blanketing.

Fireworks

24

Flickering lights
In the night sky
Rockets soar
Explosion of colour
Whistling wheels
Oohs and aahs
Remember, remember
Kids eyes wide
Sparklers sizzle

Afterthought

The last minute invite,
Or none at all.
You feel your heart,
Inside you fall.

The whispers in ears,
The roll of the eyes,
Hold your head high,
As you walk by.

Never want,
A photo with you,
Makes you feel ugly,
Sad and blue.

There for them,
At the end of the phone,
But never given,
Your own chance to moan.

Smiles to your face,
Not to your back,
Are they waiting,
To see you crack?

Inclusitivity,
Is all that is saught,
For the one that is,
The afterthought.

Tittle-Tattlers

He pushed into me,
She pushed me back,
He poked me in the eye,
Manners they do lack!

She said she hates me,
He said he's not my friend,
She looked at me meanly,
The tell-tales never end.

He kicked me in the leg,
She's being really rude,
He stole my pencil,
She spat on my food.

She laughed at my picture,
He touched my hair.
She put my hat on.
He said he doesn't care.

The trials and tribulations,
Of young children in school,
Spare a thought for teachers,
Keeping their cool!

It won't be forever

Clothes are scattered on the floor,
Stickers cover their bedroom door.

Wrappers are hidden down the sofa,
School and football, you're their chauffeur.

Dirty cups, plates and dishes,
"Feed me now," the poor cat wishes.

Water left inside the bath.
Fill the dishwasher? "Ha," they laugh.

Shoes discarded in the hall,
Cross when one inevitably falls.

Pants left inside their trousers,
Yet tidy up round their friends houses.

Embrace the chaos and the mess,
For one day they'll have flown the nest.

Football tournament

In football a nations hopes and dreams,
Rest on the shoulders of their teams.

Fans unite to cheer them on,
Friends and strangers, join as one.

A collective gasp as the ball nears the net,
A roar as they score, loud as a jet.

Tears of joy and tears of sadness,
Irrational feelings, that's football madness.

Dreams are dashed or dreams are made,
The intial hurt, in time will fade.

Then on we look to the next game,
Where the cycle will repeat again.

Football

Frenzied fans,
Ostentatious players,
Officious coaches,
Troubled prayers,
Bored ballboys,
Absurd clout,
Loquacious commentators,
Lager louts.

We Go Together

Coffee and tea,
Honey and bee.

Socks and crocs,
Keys to locks.

Pie and custard,
Honey and mustard.

Butter on toast,
Gravy on a roast.

Sausage and mash,
Casino and cash.

Fish and chips,
Crisps and dips.

Strawberries and cream,
Sports and a team.

Birds and a feather,
Couples together.

Eggs and a hen,
Paper and pen.

A ceiling of stars

A clear night sky,
Stars shine brightly,
The sheer enormity of space,
Can overwhelm.
Like tiny cracks in the ceiling,
One more crack could bring the roof,
Crashing down.
Yet they have been there,
Long, long before us.
And still will shine,
Long after we have gone.
For nature is powerful,
Nature is beautiful.
We may not always see them shine,
But the stars are always there.